Girls
wanna have fun!

FRIENDSHIP
Origami

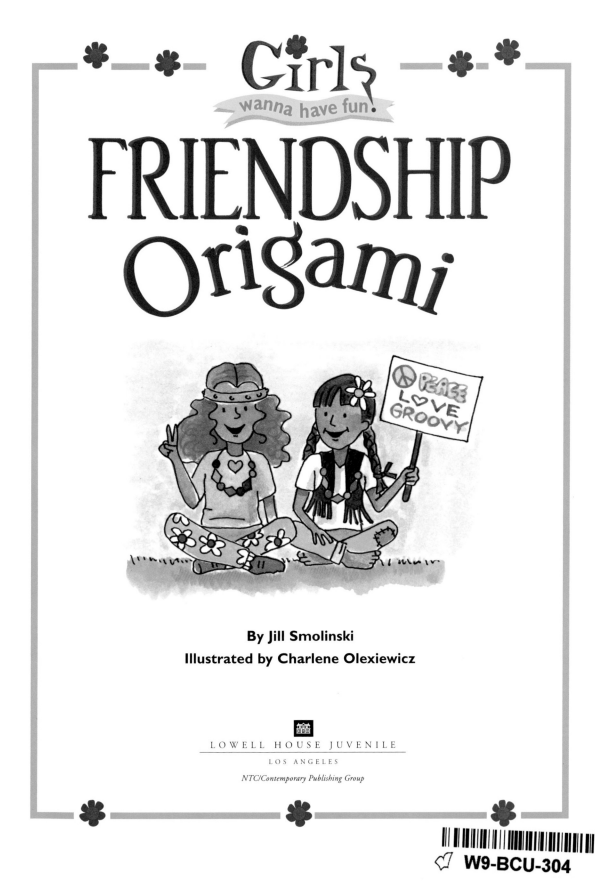

By Jill Smolinski

Illustrated by Charlene Olexiewicz

LOWELL HOUSE JUVENILE

LOS ANGELES

NTC/Contemporary Publishing Group

W9-BCU-304

Published by Lowell House
A division of NTC/Contemporary Publishing Group, Inc.
4255 West Touhy Avenue, Lincolnwood (Chicago), Illinois 60712 U.S.A.

Managing Director and Publisher: Jack Artenstein
Director of Publishing Services: Rena Copperman
Editorial Director: Brenda Pope-Ostrow
Director of Art Production: Bret Perry
Project Editor: Amy Downing
Designer: Treesha Runnells
Typesetter: Carolyn Wendt

ISBN 0-7373-9859-0

Lowell House books can be purchased at special discounts
when ordered in bulk for premiums and special sales.
Contact Customer Service at the address above,
or call 1-800-323-4900.

Printed and bound in the United States of America
PC 10 9 8 7 6 5 4 3 2 1

Contents

• • • • • • • • • •

❋ Basic Folds & Forms ❋

There are three basic folds you will use throughout this book:

Valley Fold
Fold the paper toward you.

Mountain Fold
Fold the paper away from you.

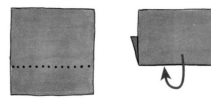

Squash Fold
This fold is usually called for when two sides of a flap need to be squashed flat. To accomplish this, poke your finger inside the flap and—you guessed it—squash it.

Many origami crafts begin with one of many basic forms. Here you'll learn the forms that are the foundation for some of the origami projects in this book.

Basic Form 1

1 Begin with a square piece of paper in a flat diamond shape, colored side facedown. Fold your paper in half, bringing the left point to meet the right point. Then unfold to make a crease.

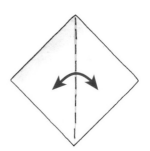

2 Fold the left and right sides to the center crease so your paper looks like a kite.

Basic Form 2

1. To make this form, begin with a square, colored side facedown. Fold your paper in half, side to side, then fold the top edge down to align with the bottom. Now open it up to the original square and fold it diagonally both ways. Reopen it.

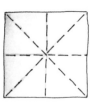

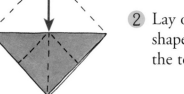

2. Fold the paper in half to make a rectangle. Then fold it in half again to make a small square. Lay the square flat on your table with the open ends facing down and to the right.

3. Now hold the top flap up straight and poke your finger inside until it reaches the very tip. Carefully squash the flap down to form a triangle. You should still be able to see part of the square from the other side. Be sure all your corners line up and look pointed. Now turn the form over and repeat this step on the other side.

Basic Form 3

1. To make this form, you must first follow Step 1 in Basic Form 2, then unfold.

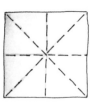

2. Lay out the origami square in front of you in a diamond shape, colored side facedown. Fold the paper in half, bringing the top point to meet the bottom point.

3. Carefully hold the right side of the form open at point A, then squash-fold it by pushing down on it to meet point B. Does it look like the illustration here?

4. Repeat Step 3 with the left side of the form.

🌸 Best Buddy Bracelet 🌸

*The pretty pattern on this bracelet makes it look tricky to fold,
but you can actually make one in just minutes.*

You Need

• 8-inch square origami paper • glue • alphabet pasta

Directions

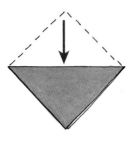

1 Begin with your square in a diamond shape, then fold it in half by bringing the top point to meet the bottom.

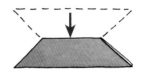

2 Fold the form in half again by bringing the top edge to meet the bottom point and creasing sharply.

3 Fold it in half again by bringing the top edge to meet the bottom.

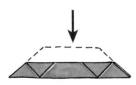

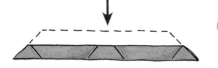

4 Fold it in half one more time top to bottom, lining up your edges carefully so they're nice and straight.

5 Now unfold your form completely, laying it flat in a diamond shape. As you can see, there are 15 creases across your form.

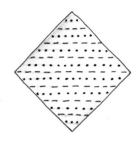

6 Refold your form, only this time use an "accordion pleat." The creases you made in Steps 1 through 4 will guide where you should fold. Follow the illustration, alternating valley folds and mountain folds to refold the form completely into an accordion pleat.

7. Do you see that you have a series of colored triangles pointing down on either side of your form? Bring the base of the triangles together by separating the center crease of the white side of the form. Your form should look like a strip with a pattern of colored squares, as shown in the illustration below.

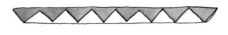

8. Put a dot of glue on one of the ends, then roll the form into a ring and tuck one end into the other to secure it.

9. Dig through the alphabet pasta to find your friend's initials and your own, then glue them to the two center squares of the bracelet.

Make a Matching Choker!

Just make two more of the bracelets following Steps 1 through 7, then tuck the end of one bracelet into the other so they form a long straight line. Use glue to hold them in place. To the other ends, attach a necklace fastener (available from craft supply stores).

❀ Secret Note Knot ❀

*Don't let the teacher catch you passing a message in this
secret note knot. It's for your friend's eyes only!*

You Need

• origami paper • pen or pencil

Directions

1 Begin with your paper in a square, colored
side down. Write a message to your friend
on the paper.

2 Now fold the left edge over
about a half inch.

3 Continue folding the left edge over and over again
as though you were rolling it. Crease it sharply each
time you fold until you have a tall thin strip.

4 Fold side A down and to the right.
To do this, you'll need to crease
the form about one-third of the
way up at a diagonal, as shown in
the illustration.

5 Now fold side A down, as shown in the illustration. (Side A should extend beyond the bottom of the form.)

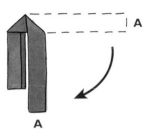

6 Fold side A to the left, as shown, and crease sharply. Uncrease. To finish tying the knot, tuck side A behind the vertical strip. Now give your friend the note knot. Make sure she knows there's a note inside so she doesn't just leave it lying around. When she's ready to read your message, she just unknots the note!

Did You Know?

This knot is not new! It was one of many paper knots boys and girls used long ago for hiding notes and sending valentines.

A *Purse*onal Touch

Does your friend have a favorite outfit? A matching purse will add just the right touch to complete her look.

You Need

- 20-inch square of origami paper (stiffer paper makes a nice sturdy purse)
- hole punch • four round reinforcement labels • markers
- 28-inch decorative rope • scissors

Directions

1. Begin with your paper in a diamond shape, colored side facing down. Make a center crease by folding the left point to meet the right, then unfolding it. Then fold your form in half by bringing the bottom point up to the top.

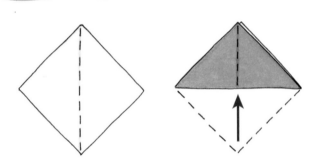

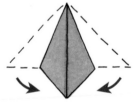

2. Fold the left edge so it lies flat against the center line (this will make the lower left corner point straight down). Repeat this step with the right edge.

3. Look closely at the illustration for this step. Fold the left bottom point up and crease it sharply, as shown in the illustration. The bottom edge of the fold you just made should not lie flat against the base of the form but should be at a slight diagonal. Unfold it, and repeat this step on the right side.

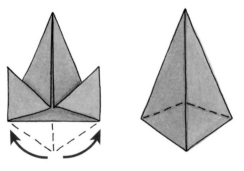

4 Now lift the left front flap so it's at a 90-degree angle from the form. Gently separate the two sides of the flap, and poke your finger inside so it touches the lower left corner of the form. The bottom left point should automatically lift up a bit. Use your other hand to push this point so it is flat and pointing upward. Repeat this step on the right side.

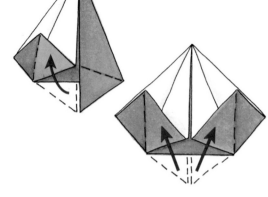

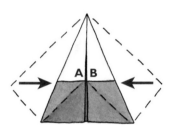

5 Turn the form over, then fold the left and right sides to the center line.

6 Do you see that it looks like a big triangle with two pockets on the front? You're going to change those pockets into triangle shapes. To do this, move point A out and to the left so it points straight up (you're not actually making a fold here, you're just shifting the direction of the point). This will automatically make the base of the front pocket move upward. Crease all the edges sharply, then repeat this step on the right side at point B.

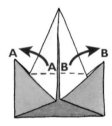

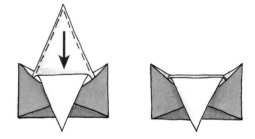

7 Fold the top point of the front flap down so it extends beyond the base of the form about 2 inches. Turn your form over and repeat this step on the other side.

8 Now use a mountain fold to bring the bottom point under so that it tucks into the front flaps. Crease sharply, then turn your form over and repeat this step on the other side.

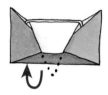

9 Open up the top of the purse and, at the same time, push in the left and right edges so they tuck inside the form. Close the purse and fold it flat. Now your purse is ready for a few finishing touches!

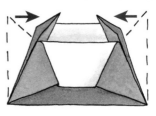

10 You might need an adult's help with this next step. Pinch the top of the purse shut to secure it, then use a hole punch to make a hole just beneath the top left corner. The hole should go through all the layers of the purse. Repeat this step on the right side.

11 Put reinforcement labels around each hole to prevent tearing. Use a marker that matches the color of your paper to color in the reinforcements.

12 To make the strap, start by cutting two 14-inch pieces of rope. Knot the end of one and string it through the front of the purse from the left side to the right, knotting the other end when you're through. Repeat this step on the back side.

Button It Up!

Looking for a cheap, easy way to add lots of style to your purse? Button it! Look for buttons that match the purse—and your friend's personality. How about buttons that are bold and bright? Or dainty and delicate? All one color? Or a crazy mix? Glue them in place on the front flap of your purse. What could be quicker . . . or cuter?

✿ Spinning Pinwheel ✿

Celebrate the good times of your friendship with a pinwheel that really works.

You Need

• two sheets origami paper, one smaller • two Popsicle® sticks
• pushpin • small piece of cork • colored masking tape

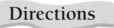

Directions

1. Start with your origami paper in a square, colored side down. Fold the paper in half by bringing the bottom edge to meet the top edge, then unfold it. Fold the form in half left to right, then unfold it.

2. Bring each corner in to meet at the center and fold.

3. Rotate the form one quarter turn so it lies as a square. Fold the form in half with the bottom meeting the top, then unfold. Fold it in half from left to right, then unfold.

4. Fold the right and left sides to meet the center line.

5. Fold the top and bottom sides to meet the center line.

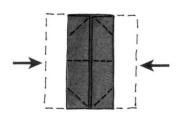

6 Make two diagonal creases across the center four squares only. To do this, fold point A to meet point B. Crease the paper sharply, then unfold it. Repeat this step on the opposite side, bringing point C to meet point D.

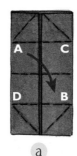
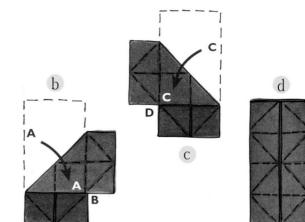

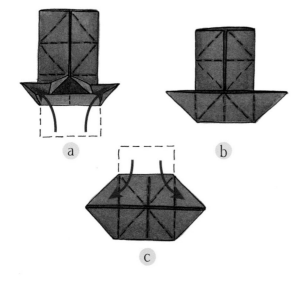

7 This next step is a little tricky, so look closely at the illustration for help. First, grasp the two bottom corners. Then lift them up and gently tug them apart so they flatten and the bottom edge meets the center. Repeat this step with the top two corners, only this time pull them down to meet the center.

8 Look at the points on the left and right sides of your form. To make a pinwheel, just take the top half of the left point and lift it so it points straight up. Then take the bottom half of the right point and pull it so it points straight down.

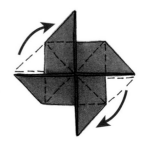

9 Now get your other sheet of paper, which should be about half the size you used to make your first pinwheel. Make another wheel by repeating Steps 1 through 8.

10 Wind tape around two Popsicle® sticks stacked end to end to cover them, and join them together to make a long handle.

11 Lay the small form on top of the big one. Secure them both to the handle by sticking a pushpin through their centers, through the Popsicle stick, and finally into the small piece of cork. The pushpin should be covered in the cork to keep you from getting poked. Now you're ready to pucker up . . . and blow!

Colors of the Season

Create your pinwheel in the right hues for the holidays. For the Fourth of July, how about red and blue? You might try orange and black for Halloween, blue and white for Hanukkah—or fold a pinwheel in your school colors to help make the time in class pass a little faster.

❀ Super Easy Earrings ❀

Your friends won't believe these earrings are made from paper!

You Need

- two matching 1½-inch squares of origami paper
- earring wires (available at craft supply stores) • straight pin

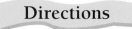

Directions

1. Begin with one of your pieces of paper in a diamond shape, white side facing up. Fold the form in half by bringing the top point to the bottom, then in half again by bringing the left point to the right. Crease well, then unfold.

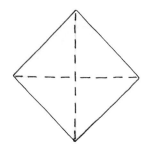

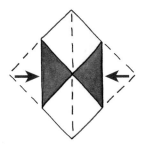

2. Fold the left and right points to the center line.

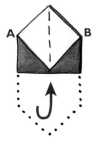

3. Fold the form in half by using a mountain fold to bring the bottom fold up to meet the top.

4. Fold point A (front flaps only) forward so it forms a diagonal edge from the bottom left point to the top point. Repeat this step with point B, then turn the form over and repeat this entire step on the other side.

5 This next step is easy as long as you follow the illustration closely. Grasp points C and D and pull them straight down. This will cause the flaps on either side of your form to straighten out—which is exactly what should happen!

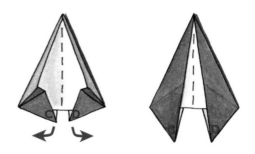

6 To make the second earring, repeat Steps 1 through 5 with the other piece of paper.

7 Ask a parent to help you with this next step. Use a straight pin to poke a tiny hole just below the top point of each earring. Then thread the wires through. That was so easy, you'll probably want to make another pair for yourself!

Add Some Shine

Want your earrings to look like real precious metals? Fold them using gold or silver foil origami paper or gift wrap! If you had your heart set on colored paper, you can still add plenty of shimmer—and make the earrings even more sturdy—by spraying shellac on the folded earrings before you put the wires in.

Friendship Flower

She likes me . . . she likes me not . . .
Here's a flower that will have your friend plucking petals
to find out why she's so special to you.

You Need

• 10-inch square of origami paper (anything smaller gets too thick to fold)
• pen or marker

Directions

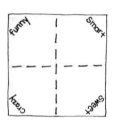

1. Begin with your paper in a square (white side facing up if you're using dual colored paper). Fold the paper in half from side to side, then top to bottom to form vertical and horizontal creases. Then reopen it into a square.

2. In each corner, write a word that describes your friend, such as *funny, smart, sweet,* or *crazy.* Be sure to write with tiny letters in the very point of each corner and use your neatest penmanship. Fold each corner point to the center of the form.

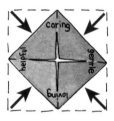

3. Write a word in each corner again. This time you'll notice that the words will cross over an opening between the two flaps of each triangle. Fold each corner point to the center of the form.

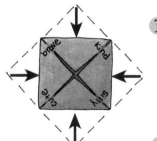

4. Think of four more words, and write one in each of the corners. Again, fold each corner to the center of the form.

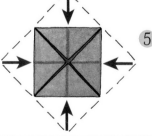

5. Turn the form over and fold each corner to the center of the form one more time, and your flower is finished. Right now it looks like a square because it will be up to your friend to make it "bloom."

6 Give the flower to your friend, and tell her to hold the form with the square (not triangle) shapes facing up. (Remember that the side with the triangle shapes is the bottom.) She should fold back the four corner points at the center toward the outside and crease. This will create the first four petals and expose four words.

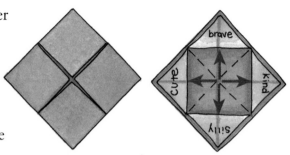

7 Tell her to pinch all four main corners (not the petals) toward the back. This will cause the center of the flower to pop up. All she needs to do is peel back the remaining two layers of petals to expose the rest of the words. Her friendship flower is now in full bloom!

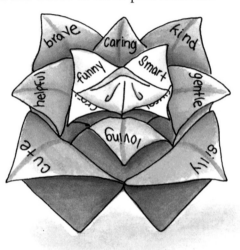

Lily Pad

This type of flower is called a lotus blossom, and you'll often find them floating in water on a lily pad. You can easily make a pad to set a lotus blossom on. Just cut a circle about twice the size of your flower from green poster board. Then snip a triangle out of it, as though you were cutting out a piece of pie. Dot the pad with a few drops of crystal glitter puff paint to look like water droplets. Place the flower on top of the lily pad. What a wonderful display of your friendship!

❀ Sweets for a Sweetie ❀

*This cute candy dish can also be used to hold paper clips,
earrings, or other tiny treasures.*

You Need

• origami paper

Directions

1. Begin with your paper in a square, colored side facing up. Fold the paper in half from side to side, then top to bottom to form vertical and horizontal creases. Then reopen it into a square.

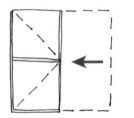

2. Fold each corner point to the center of the form.

3. Turn your form over, then fold each corner point to the center again.

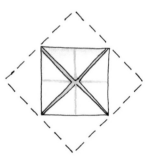

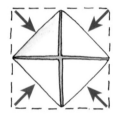

4. Fold the form in half by bringing the right side to meet the left, then unfold.

5. Fold the paper in half from bottom to top.

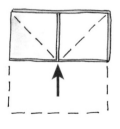

6 It's time to push the candy dish into shape. Use your right thumb and index finger to "pinch" the bottom right of the form, just underneath the square flaps. Use your left hand to pinch the other side. Now push your hands toward each other as you bring the right and left upper corners to the center.

7 Just turn the form over, and you have a dish with four little pockets for candy.

A Playful Puppet

This same form can be used to make an adorable animal puppet! Start with your paper colored side down, and follow Steps 1 through 6. Then glue the top and bottom quarters of the form together (as though you were putting glue between your two index fingers and two thumbs). Use a mountain fold to fold back the bottom corners to "round out" your puppet's face. The top points are the ears. Use markers to draw on facial features, and it's show time!

✿ Frame It Up ✿

Turn a simple photo into a super nifty gift by presenting it in a paper frame you make yourself.

You Need

- 8-inch square of origami paper • glue • beads or buttons
- photo, about $3\frac{1}{2}$ inches square

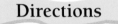

Directions

1. Begin with your paper in a square, colored side facing up. Fold the paper in half from side to side, then top to bottom to form vertical and horizontal creases. Reopen it into a square.

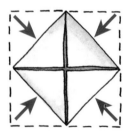

2. Fold each corner point to the center of the form.

3. Turn your form over, then fold each corner point to the center again.

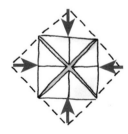

4. Turn the form over again, and you'll see that it now has four square flaps with points that meet in the center. Use a valley fold to fold each inside point back to its outside corner. Run your finger along the fold to make a firm crease at the base of each of the little triangles. The front of your frame is complete!

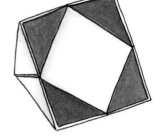

5. Your frame will be able to stand on its own if you just reach back and unfold the triangle-shaped flaps on the left and right sides so they stand straight out. Set your frame down to see how it rests on the bottom edges of these flaps.

6. Glue beads or other decorations on the frame's front corners. Slide the photo into the frame so each of its corners rests underneath a corner flap.

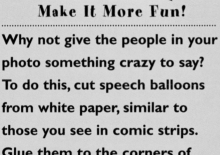

Make It More Fun!

Why not give the people in your photo something crazy to say? To do this, cut speech balloons from white paper, similar to those you see in comic strips. Glue them to the corners of your frame. Then write in silly sayings, such as "Are we cute, or what?" or "Help! I've been framed!"

✿ Ring-Around-a-Finger! ✿

*One piece of paper makes a trio of rings—
enough for you and two of your buddies.*

You Need

- 4½-inch square of origami paper • scissors • clear tape
- assorted charms and/or beads • strong craft glue

Directions

1. Begin by cutting a piece of origami paper into three equal pieces. Each piece will be 4½ inches long and 1½ inches wide. You need one-third sheet for each ring you make.

2. With the colored side down, fold one of the pieces of paper in half by bringing the top edge to meet the bottom, then unfold. Fold the top and bottom edges to the center line.

3. Now fold the form in half by bringing the bottom edge up to meet the top.

4. Fold the lower right corner to the top of the form, crease it, then unfold.

5. Use a valley fold to fold the right side over to form a square. A diagonal crease from the last step should run through it.

6. Fold the right side over again, crease sharply, then fold over once more. Unfold.

7. Use a mountain fold to bring the right edge back and up.

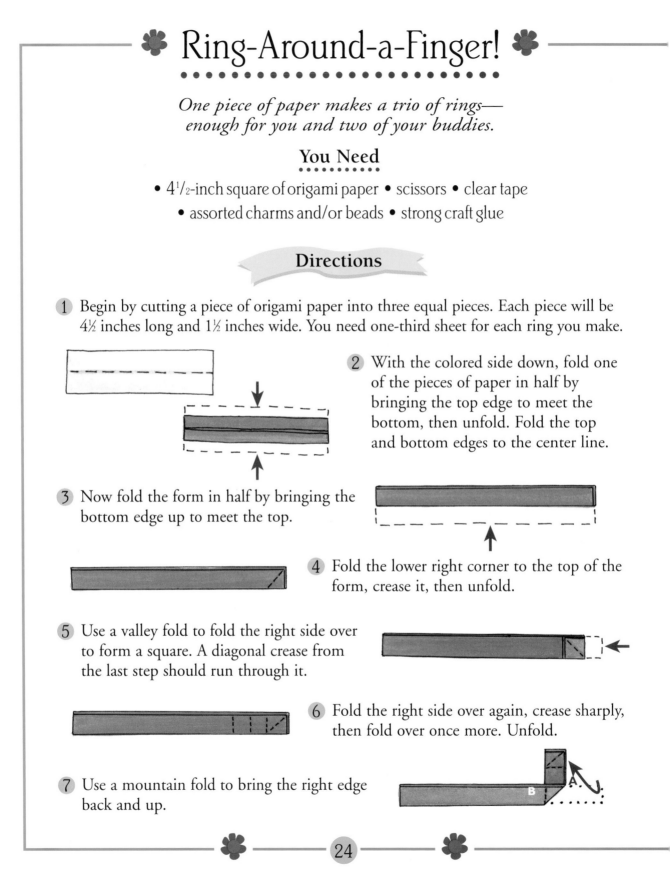

8 Now use a mountain fold to bring point A to point B. Your paper should look like an *L* on its side.

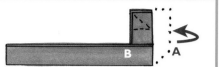

9 Fold to bring the top edge of the *L* down.

10 Turn the form over. Look for the thick triangle at the back of your ring, fold the top edge down, and tuck it into the triangle.

11 Finally, fold back the two corners into a point at the other end of the strip, curl it around, and tuck it into the open end of the square. Fit the ring on the finger you wish to wear it, tightening it so you can still take it on and off. With a small, clear piece of tape, secure the end to the ring. If your ring is too large, cut some length off the long end of the strip before you tuck it in.

12 Select a charm or bead for your ring. If the ring is for a friend, choose one that matches her personality. Glue it onto the ring using strong craft glue. Allow to dry. Once your friend sees this adorable personalized ring, she'll want to make one, too!

MY FAVORITE KINDS OF RINGS... ONION RINGS, CIRCUS RINGS, TELEPHONE RINGS (WHEN IT'S FOR ME!)

Make It More Fun!

As your collection of rings grows, try stringing the rings onto a colorful plastic cord or length of yarn, making them into a friendship necklace.

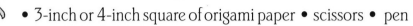

*Show a pal she has all the "write" stuff with
a pen that has a pretty flower perched on top.*

You Need

- 3-inch or 4-inch square of origami paper • scissors • pen
- clear tape • green paper • green florist tape

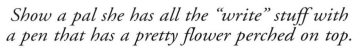

Directions

1. Start with Basic Form 3. Make sure the open ends are pointed upward, away from you.

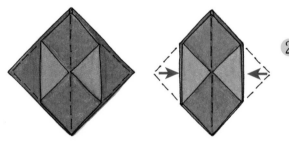

2. Find the points on the right and left sides (front flap only), and fold them to the center line. Turn over and repeat this step on the other side.

3. Use a valley fold to fold each lower corner as shown here, making sure the points just touch in the middle. Turn your form over and repeat on the other side.

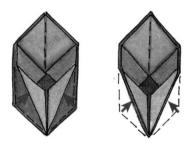

4. Use your scissors to cut straight across the bottom to make a tiny hole.

5 Now you're ready to let your flower bloom! Gently tug the petals open. Bend each one back and crease. Poke your finger inside the middle of the flower so the petals no longer meet in the center.

6 Insert the top of the pen slightly into the bottom of the flower. Cut leaves out of green paper, lay them at the base of the flower, and tape everything in place. Then wrap green florist tape around the pen—of course, leaving the point exposed so the pen still works.

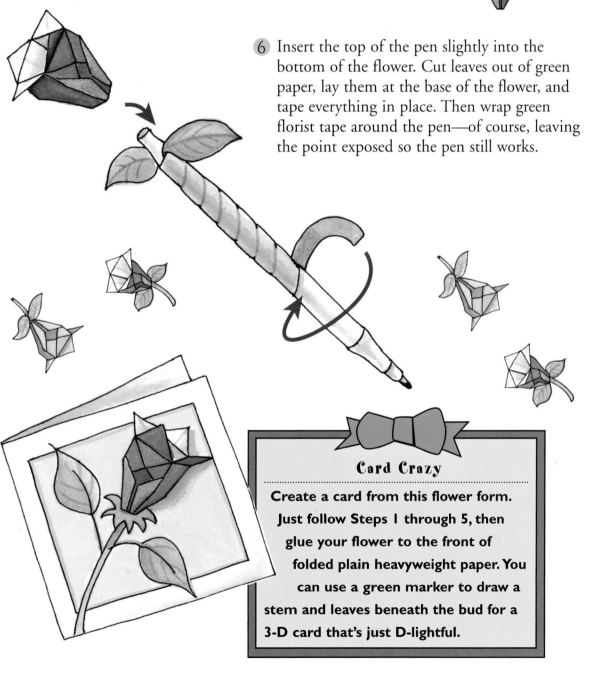

Card Crazy

Create a card from this flower form. Just follow Steps 1 through 5, then glue your flower to the front of folded plain heavyweight paper. You can use a green marker to draw a stem and leaves beneath the bud for a 3-D card that's just D-lightful.

❀ Groovy Love Beads ❀

*Let a pal know that you've got a "groovy" kind of
friendship by giving her a string of origami love beads.
They're far out!*

You Need

- two 1½-inch squares of different colored paper (for each bead) • glue
- scissors • assorted plastic beads and charms • plastic threading wire

Directions

1 Begin with Basic Form 2, then fold the left
and right points downward (front flap
only). The sides should lie flat against
the center line. Turn the form over
and repeat this on the other side.
You've just completed half a bead!

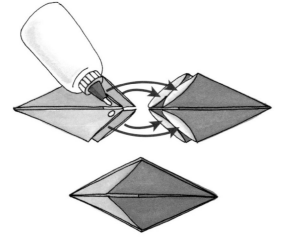

2 Repeat Step 1 with another piece of
paper. Lay each form flat so the
bottom points face each other. You'll
see that each form has "pockets" at
the bottom. Put a dab of glue on
the points of the left form, then
slide them into the pockets of the
form on the right.

3 Lift the top point (front flap only) at a right angle
from the form. Turn it over and repeat this step on
the other side.

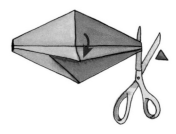

4 Use scissors to snip off the tips of the left and right
points. That's it!

5 Cut a piece of plastic threading wire about 2 feet long. Poke one end of the wire into the right side of your bead, through the center, and out the left side.

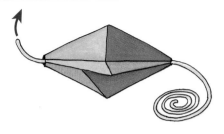

6 Make as many beads as you want, following Steps 1 through 5. String them together, alternating an origami bead with a plastic bead or charm. When you're finished, knot the ends of the wire together. Leave a bit of empty space near the neck area, and you've got it right . . . that is, *right on!*

Beaded Streamer

Think big, and fold up some beads using 5-inch or larger origami paper. String them together to make a beaded curtain to hang over a window or doorway. Tube-shaped dry pasta makes a great substitute for the plastic beads.

The perfect gift for a friend you'll always remember—a handy holder that'll help her remember where she puts all those little items like pencils, pins, or even precious keepsakes.

You Need

- origami paper • scissors • poster board
- glue • tape • rickrack trim

Directions

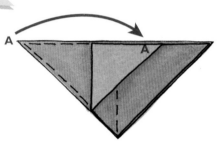

1. Begin with Basic Form 2, and place the form so that the open end is on top. Fold point A over (front flap only) so that it touches the top edge of the form about halfway between the center and the right side. Crease sharply.

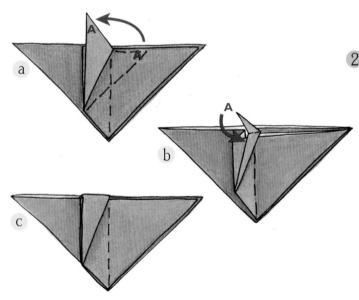

a

b

c

2. Now fold point A up so it points straight up, as shown in the illustration. Tuck point A inside the top of the form, making sure it is placed inside the top single layer only. (Do not catch the "pleat" located inside.)

3. Repeat Steps 1 and 2 on the right side of the form.

4 Turn the form over and repeat Steps 1 through 3 on the other side. Your form should look like the one shown here.

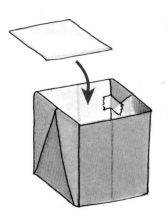

5 Gently slip your finger inside and open the holder while flattening and squaring out the base at the bottom.

6 To strengthen the bottom of the container, cut a square out of cardboard slightly smaller than the base. Put a dab of glue on the square and slip it into the origami holder, glue side down. To strengthen the sides, place a piece of tape on each inside corner.

7 Trim the top and bottom edges with rickrack, and fill the box with pencils, cotton swabs, or even tiny treasures.

Stack It!

You can fold a bunch of boxes that stack neatly inside each other—an inexpensive yet special gift idea! Use paper in assorted colors, starting with a 4-inch square and increasing the size of the paper by an inch for each additional catchall container.

✿ Oh, Baby! ✿

Your friends will go "gaga" over this adorable doll who's snuggled sweetly in a blanket.

You Need

• origami paper • colored pencils • glue • pastel colored button with raised threading hole • scissors • pipe cleaner • extra paper

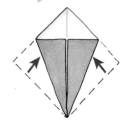

Directions

1 Begin by completing Basic Form 1.

2 Use a mountain fold to fold back the top point.

3 Fold the upper left and right points so they meet at the center line. Turn your form over.

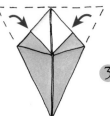

4 Do you see the diamond shape at the top of your form? That's the doll's head. To wrap the blanket tightly around the baby, lift the head up slightly so you can fold points A and B to the center.

5 Round out your doll's head by using mountain folds to fold back the top and bottom points. Fold back the point at the bottom of the blanket, and your form is complete.

6 Use colored pencils to draw eyes, nose, and pink cheeks. Give your baby a pacifier by gluing the button, "bump" side up, to the baby's mouth. Then cut a 2-inch strip of pipe cleaner, curl it around a pencil, and glue it to the top of the baby's head. Add a teeny, tiny bow cut from paper.